Collins

easy learning

Handwriting bumper book

Ages 5–7

My birthday is on

Karina Law

How to use this book

- Easy Learning bumper books help your child improve basic skills, build confidence and develop a love of learning.
- Find a quiet, comfortable place to work, away from distractions.
- Get into a routine of completing one or two bumper book pages with your child every day.
- Ask your child to circle the star that matches how many activities they have completed every two pages:

Some = half of the activities   Most = more than half   All = all the activities

- The progress certificate at the back of this book will help you and your child keep track of how many ⭐ have been circled.
- Encourage your child to work through all of the activities eventually, and praise them for completing the progress certificate.

Parent tip
Look out for tips on how to help your child with handwriting practice.

- Help your child to rest their pencil in the 'V' between their thumb and index finger; their fingers should be between one and two centimetres away from the pencil tip.
- Introduce your child to the 'starting point' in each activity, where they should first place their pencil or pen on the paper.
- If your child is left-handed, check with your child's school to find out how they teach letter formation; some of the strokes will be made in the opposite direction to right-handed writers.
- The National Curriculum states that children should be taught to understand which letters, when next to one another, are best left unjoined. These are called break letters. Some schools do teach children to join some, or all these letters. Check which handwriting style your child's school uses.

- Ask your child to find and colour the little monkeys that are hidden throughout this book.
- This will help engage them with the pages of the book and get them interested in the activities.

(Don't count this one.)

Published by Collins
An imprint of HarperCollinsPublishers Ltd
The News Building
1 London Bridge Street
London
SE1 9GF

Browse the complete Collins catalogue at collins.co.uk

© HarperCollinsPublishers Ltd 2011
This edition © HarperCollinsPublishers Ltd 2015

10 9 8

ISBN 978-0-00-815147-8

The author asserts the moral right to be identified as the author of this work.

British Library Cataloguing in Publication Data.

A Catalogue record for this publication is available from the British Library.

Written by Karina Law
Based on content by Sue Peet
Design and layout by Linda Miles, Lodestone Publishing and Contentra Technologies Ltd

Illustrated by Graham Smith, Andy Tudor, Peter Bull Art Studio and Jenny Tulip
Cover design by Sarah Duxbury and Paul Oates
Cover illustration by Jenny Tulip and Kathy Baxendale
Project managed by Sonia Dawkins

FSC™
MIX
Paper from responsible source
www.fsc.org
FSC™ C007454

This book is produced from independently certified FSC™ paper to ensure responsible forest management.

For more information visit: www.harpercollins.co.uk/green

Contents

i is for insect

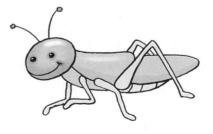

Patterns: Spider bungee jump

1 Draw over the broken lines to make four spider threads. Start at the green dot.

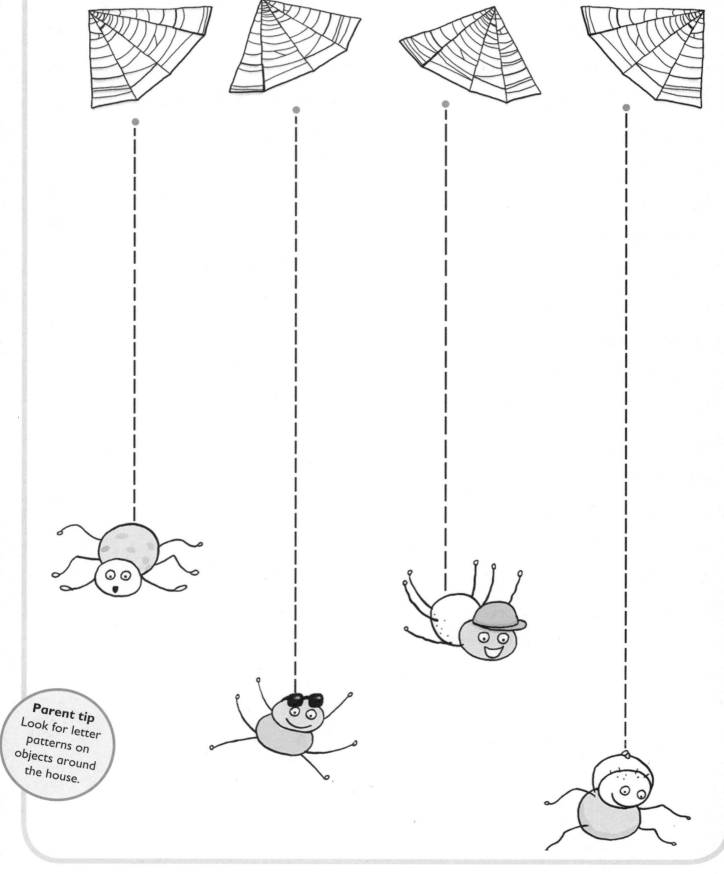

Parent tip
Look for letter patterns on objects around the house.

Patterns: Jump for it!

2 Trace over the broken lines to help the frog hop across the river past the hungry crocodiles. Start at the green dot.

Patterns: Bouncing beach balls

1 Draw over the broken lines to show how the four balls bounce. Start at the green dot.

Patterns: Letter shapes

2 Draw over the broken lines to complete the patterns. Start at the green dot.

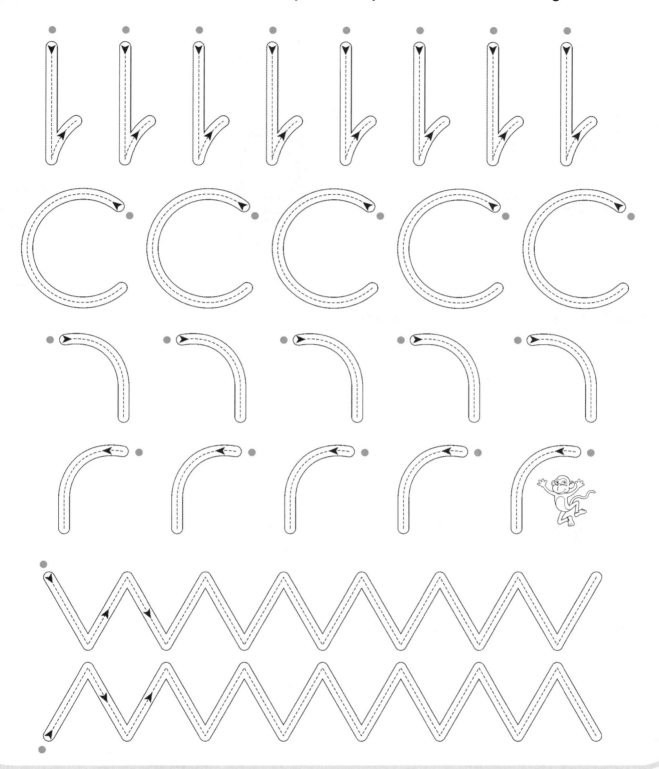

Letter shapes: l, i, t

1 Trace and write. Start at the green dot.

Trace the grey letter l.

l is for lion

Parent tip
Encourage your child to use their non-writing hand to hold the page steady.

2 Trace and write. Start at the green dot.

Trace the grey letter i.

i is for insect

3 Trace and write. Start at the green dot.

Trace the grey letter t.

t is for tiger

4 Practise writing l in this sentence.

All lions like to lunch.

5 Practise writing i in this sentence.

Tiger Tim is feeling ill.

6 Draw round the teddy, beginning at the green dot. Write t on his tummy.

Letter shapes: u, j, y

1 Trace and write. Start at the green dot.

u   u   u

Trace the grey letter u.

u is for umbrella

2 Trace and write. Start at the green dot.

j   j   j

Trace the grey letter j.

j is for jam jar

3 Trace and write. Start at the green dot.

y   y   y

Trace the grey letter y.

y is for yo-yo

4 Practise writing u in this sentence.

Huddle under an umbrella.

5 Practise writing j in this sentence.

We enjoy jogging.

6 Practise writing y in this sentence.

A yawning yak.

How much did you do?   Activities 1–6

Circle the star
to show what
you have done.

 Some   Most   All

Letter shapes: r, n, h, b

1 Trace and write. Start at the green dot.

r r r

Trace the grey letter r.

r is for ruler

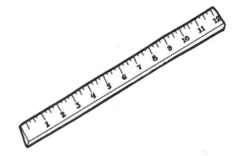

2 Trace and write. Start at the green dot.

n n n

Trace the grey letter n.

n is for nose

Parent tip
Try making letter shapes out of play dough or clay with your child.

3 Trace and write. Start at the green dot.

h h h

Trace the grey letter h.

h is for house

4 Trace and write. Start at the green dot.

Trace the grey letter b.

b is for bear

5 Practise writing r, n, h and b in this sentence.

Nine brown hens running backwards.

How much did you do?   ## Activities 1–5

Circle the star
to show what
you have done.

  Some

  Most

  All

13

Letter shapes: m, k, p

1 Trace and write. Start at the green dot.

Trace the grey letter m.

m is for mouse

2 Trace and write. Start at the green dot.

Trace the grey letter k.

k is for koala

3 Trace and write. Start at the green dot.

Trace the grey letter p.

p is for pencil

4 Practise writing m in this sentence.

A monkey jumping on a trampoline.

5 Practise writing k and p in this sentence.

A pair of kangaroos hopping on pogo sticks.

How much did you do?   **Activities 1–5**

Circle the star
to show what
you have done.

 Some

 Most

 All

15

Letter shapes: c, a, o, d

1 Trace and write. Start at the green dot.

c c c

Trace the grey letter c.

c is for clock

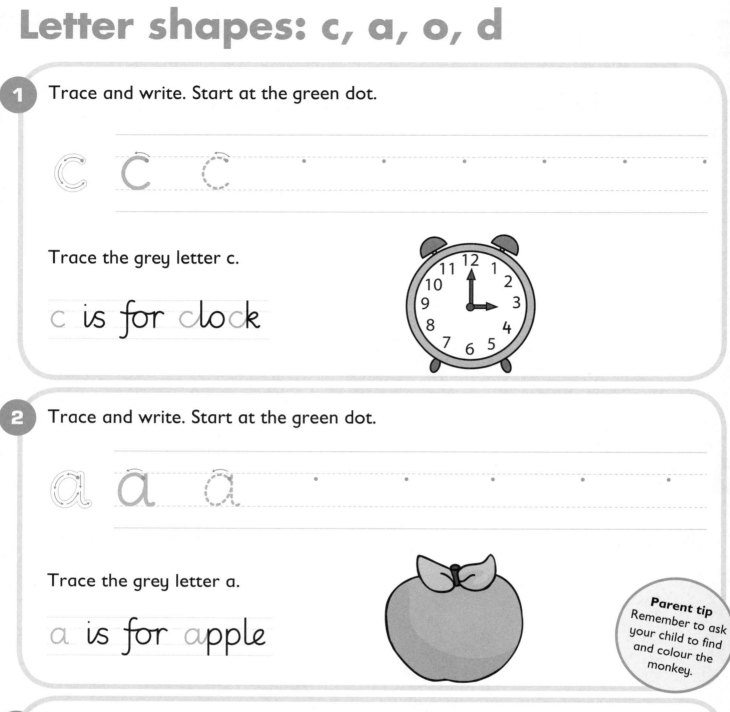

2 Trace and write. Start at the green dot.

a a a

Trace the grey letter a.

a is for apple

Parent tip
Remember to ask your child to find and colour the monkey.

3 Trace and write. Start at the green dot.

o o o

Trace the grey letter o.

o is for octopus

4 Trace and write. Start at the green dot.

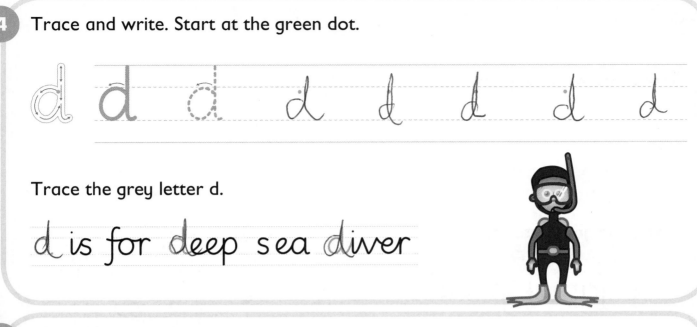

Trace the grey letter d.

d is for deep sea diver

5 Practise writing c in this sentence.

Five scared mice caught by a crafty cat.

6 Practise writing d in this sentence.

A duo of daintily dancing dinosaurs.

How much did you do?   **Activities 1–6**

Circle the star
to show what
you have done.

 Some

 Most

 All

Letter shapes: e, g, q, f, s

1 Trace and write. Start at the green dot.

e e e · · · · ·

Trace the grey letter e.

e is for elephant

2 Trace and write. Start at the green dot.

g g g · · · · ·

Trace the grey letter g.

g is for goat

3 Trace and write. Start at the green dot.

q q q · · · · ·

Trace the grey letter q.

q is for queen

4 Trace and write. Start at the green dot.

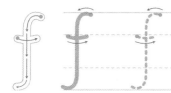

Trace the grey letter f.

f is for fairy

5 Trace and write. Start at the green dot.

Trace the grey letter s.

s is for strawberry

6 Practise writing f in this sentence.

A frog hops after a fly.

How much did you do?   Activities 1–6

Circle the star
to show what
you have done.

 Some   Most   All

Letter shapes: v, w, x, z

---

1 Trace and write. Start at the green dot.

Trace the grey letter v.

v is for vase

---

2 Trace and write. Start at the green dot.

Trace the grey letter w.

w is for whale

---

3 Trace and write. Start at the green dot.

Trace the grey letter x.

x is for x-ray

---

4 Trace and write. Start at the green dot.

Trace the grey letter z.

z is for zebra

5 Practise writing x in these words.

Six foxes in boxes.

6 Practise writing z these words.

Snoozing zebras.

Letter joins: short vowel a

1 Trace and write.

 bat   bat

 rat   rat

 cap   cap

 tap   tap

 bag   bag

 van   van

Cat on a mat.

Cat on a mat

22

Letter joins: short vowel e

2 Trace and write.

 pen   pen

 hen   hen

 ten   ten

 legs   legs

 bed   bed

web   web

Little red hen.

Little red hen.

How much did you do?

Circle the star to show what you have done.

 Some

 Most

 All

Activities 1–2

23

Letter joins: short vowel i

Parent tip
Write other practice words and sentences on a piece of paper for your child to copy.

1 Trace and write.

zip   zip

ship   ship

bin   bin

pin   pin

fish   fish

dish   dish

Jack and Jill went up the hill.

Jack and Jill went up the hill.

Letter joins: short vowel o

Trace and write.

dog dog

log log

cot cot

mop mop

shop shop

sock sock

Fox on a box.

Fox on a box.

Letter joins: short vowel u

Parent tip
Let your child use different writing tools to practise letter joins – paint, crayons, marker pens or glitter pens.

1 Trace and write.

 sun sun

 bun bun

 jug jug

 mug mug

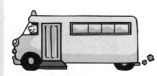 bug bug

 bus bus

A duck in a cup.

A duck in a cup

Letter joins: ch and th

2 Trace and write.

ch   *ch*   *ch*

th   *th*   *th*

chain   *chain*

chips   *chips*

chair   *chair*

thumb   *thumb*

three   *three*

think   *think*

Capital letters

Capital letters don't join to any other letter.
Trace and write. Start at the green dot.

A A

B B

C C

D D

E E

F F

G G

H H

Parent tip
Point out street signs printed with capital letters to your child.

2 Trace and write these capital letters.

I I

J J

K K

L L

M M

N N

O O

P P

Q Q

Capital letters

1 Trace and write these capitals letters to complete the alphabet.

R R R R R R R

S S S S S S

T T T

U U U

V V V

W W W

X X X

Y Y Y

Z Z Z

Capital letters: parcel sort

2 Choose different friends to give each gift to. Write their names on the labels. Remember to use a capital letter at the start of each name.

Jobs

1 Read these jokes and copy them in your neatest handwriting.

Why did the sparrow fly into the library?

It was looking for bookworms.

Where do sick horses go?

To a horse-pital!

What's a cat's favourite colour?

Purrr-ple!

Parent tip
Help your child find more jokes from a book or the internet to copy out.

Handwriting practice: 'Ip dip dip'

2 Write this poem in your best handwriting.

Ip dip dip

My blue ship,

Sailing on the water

Like a cup and saucer.

How much did you do?   Activities 1–2

Circle the star to show what you have done.

 Some

 Most

 All

Numbers

1 Trace over each number, then write it out. Start at the green dot.

1 1 1 1 1 1 1 1 1 1 1 1 2 2 2 2 2 2

3 3 3 3 3 3 3 3 3 4 4 4 4 4 4

5 5 5 5 5 5 5 5 6 6 6 6 6 6

7 7 7 7 7 7 7 7 8 8 8 8 8 8 8 8

9 9 9 9 9 9 9 9 10 10 10 10 10

2 Trace over each word, then write it out. Start at the green dot.

one one one two two

three three four four

five five six six

seven seven eight eight

nine nine ten ten

Copy the number poem in your neatest handwriting.

One for sorrow *Ones or sorrow*

Two for joy *Two for joy*

Parent tip
Call out numbers in a random order and ask your child to write them down.

Three for a girl *Tree s or a girl*

Four for a boy *For a boy*

Five for silver *sive for silver*

Six for gold *six for gold*

Seven for a secret, never to be told. *Sev ta for a sect Never to bu told*

How much did you do? ## Activities 1–3

Circle the star
to show what
you have done.

 Some

 Most

 All

Alphabet practice: School register

1 Trace over each capital letter. Start at the green dot.

A B C D E F G H I J K L M

N O P Q R S T U V W X Y Z

2 Read the names below and on page 37, then copy each one. Then write them out again in alphabetical order on the right-hand side of these pages. Remember that capital letters do not join to any other letter.

Harry		Ahmed
Chloe		
William		
Ronan		
Mamoun		
Danny		
Xavier		
Georgia		
Poppy		
Ahmed		
Oscar		

3

Tamsin
James
Zachary
Bradley
Kiran
Umar
Violet
Nikita
Finley
Imogen
Quentin
Yasmin
Ella
Lola
Sammy

Parent tip
Ask your child to make a 'register' of their friends in alphabetical order.

How much did you do?　　**Activities 1–3**

Circle the star to show what you have done.

 Some　　 Most　　 All

Alliteration: Alphabet zoo

Parent tip
Help your child to think up and write tongue twisters using alliteration.

1 Alliteration is when words beginning with the same sound are used close together. Read and write.

Angry alligators annoying ants.

Badgers baking biscuits.

Cross camels in canoes.

Dinosaurs dunking doughnuts.

Elephants exercising energetically.

Fat frogs frightening fish.

Greedy geese gobbling grapes.

Hairy hamsters hiding in hats.

2 Read and write.

Jumpy jackals playing judo.

Keen kangaroos flying kites.

Lions looking at leaflets.

Monkeys making a mess.

Newts nibbling insects.

Octopuses wearing odd socks.

Pandas playing Pass the Parcel.

1 **Read and write.**

Squirrels quarrelling quietly.

Rabbits reading recipes.

Snakes sneaking into sleeping bags.

Tigers talking on the telephone.

Ugly bugs under an umbrella.

Vultures eating vegetables.

Young yaks yodelling.

Zebras zipping round the zoo.

Handwriting practice: 'The swan'

Copy this poem in your neatest handwriting.

Swan swam over the sea,

Swim, swan, swim!

Swan swam back again,

Well swum, swan!

Anon

How much did you do? | **Activities 1–2**

Circle the star
to show what
you have done.

Some   Most   All

Word endings: ful, y, less

1 Adjectives are describing words. Some words can be changed into adjectives by adding ful, y or less at the end.
Write ful at the end of each word below. Then write out the whole word twice.

hopeful

care

forget

help

cheer

delight

use

truth

peace

play

Parent tip
Help your child to think of and write down other words that can be changed with these word endings.

2 Look at the words ending in y below. Choose the best word to write below each picture.

rainy   sleepy   windy   crunchy

_____   _____   _____   _____

3 Write less at the end of each word. Then write out the whole word twice.

careless

end

speech

fear

hope

help

harm

use

Group names

Look at the words below. Write each word under the correct group name. One has been done for you.

pink pineapple daisy melon ~~ladybird~~

rabbit rose blue ~~beetle~~ goldfish pear

daffodil hamster yellow snowdrop

white banana ~~bee~~ gerbil fly

Fruit

pineapple

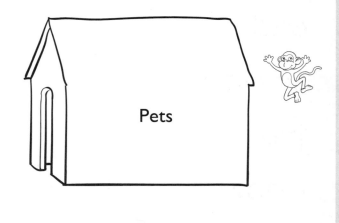

Pets

2 Look at the words on page 44. Write each word under the correct group name.

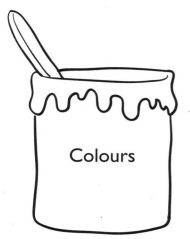

Colours

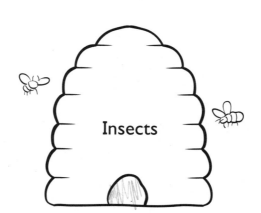

Insects

Flowers

_____

_____

_____

_____

_____

_____

_____

_____

_____

_____

_____

_____

Parent tip
Use the internet to find other 'group words' such as toys, trees or shapes, then ask your child to write them down.

Word endings: ing

1 Read and copy the words ending in ing below.

eating

dancing

bouncing

crawling

crying

jumping

yawning

blowing

sleeping

singing

flying

2 Look at the words on page 46 again. Write the correct word below each picture.

How much did you do?   Activities 1–2

Circle the star
to show what
you have done.

☆ Some   ★ Most   ★ All

47

Action words

Copy the ideas in this list of things to do on a rainy day. Put a tick next to the ideas you like best.

Bake some biscuits.

Learn a magic trick.

Plant some vegetables.

Make a den.

Perform a puppet show.

Try a new food.

Watch a film with my family.

Interview a member of my family.

2 Think of two more 'rainy day ideas' and write them down.

_____

_____

Parent tip
Help your child to write ideas for rainy days on 'tickets' to be kept in a bag or box. Pick out an idea next time it rains!

3 Draw a line to match these action words with an ending to help you get ready for your holiday. Then write out each instruction in full.

Have	a book
Find	suncream
Buy	a haircut
Choose	my flip flops
Look for	my suitcase
Pack	a bucket and spade

_____

_____

_____

_____

_____

How much did you do?   **Activities 1-3**

Circle the star to show what you have done.

Some   Most   All

49

Past tense

1 When we write about something that has already happened, we use the past tense. Read and write.

Yesterday I...

bounced on my bed

visited a volcano

zoomed around a zoo

juggled with jelly

met a magician

ate an apple

hugged a hedgehog

2 Read and write.

Parent tip
Ask your child to write a list of things they are doing today in the present tense.

kissed a koala

travelled in a train

nibbled a nut

painted a parrot

waved a wand

escaped from an elephant

lost a library book

How much did you do?   **Activities 1–2**

Circle the star
to show what
you have done.

 Some

Most

 All

Word endings: le

1 Trace the letters. Start at the green dot.

le le le le le le le le le le le le le le

2 Read these words ending in le. Then write each one out three times.

table

apple

candle

bottle

beetle

needle

trifle

uncle

cycle

turtle

Parts of the body

Look at the words below. Copy the words. Then draw lines from each word to the correct body part.

forehead knee elbow thumb neck foot ankle
waist arm chest heel finger shoulder ear

Parent tip
Name other parts of the body and ask your child to write them down.

How much did you do?

Activities 1–3

Circle the star to show what you have done.

 Some

 Most

 All

Shape words

Look at the shape words below. Write each word in the correct shape.

square triangle rectangle
hexagon circle star

2 Look at the shape words below. Write the word below the correct shape.

cube cuboid pyramid sphere cone cylinder

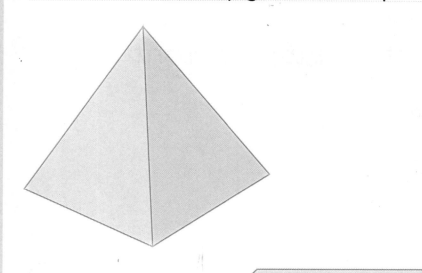

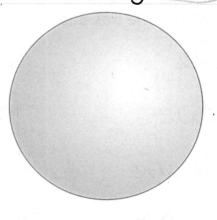

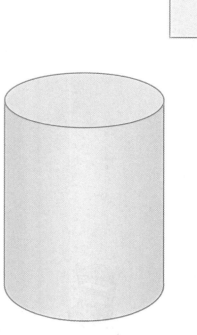

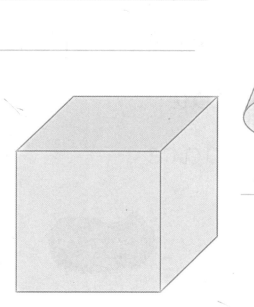

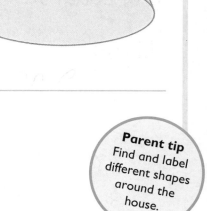

How much did you do?   **Activities 1–2**

Circle the star to show what you have done.

 Some

 Most

 All

Rhyming words

1 Join each word to a rhyming word. Then write each rhyming pair.
The first one has been done for you.

kite	cheat	kite bright
shoe	joke	
please	leaf	
ghost	blue	
sweet	gate	
chair	bright	
whale	toast	
cloak	cheese	
straight	tail	
thief	dare	

2 Find pairs of rhyming words in the box and write them inside the bubbles.

house	hole	delay	zip
ship	away	mouse	mole

Parent tip
Make cards with rhyming words on them. Play a game of snap with rhyming pairs.

How much did you do?   Activities 1–2

Circle the star to show what you have done.

 Some   Most    All

57

More group names

Look at the words below. Write each word under the correct group name.
One has been done for you.

helicopter broccoli bucket tennis

rainbow football sand aeroplane

hail bus waves hurricane peas

gymnastics crab tram badminton

snow carrot sweetcorn

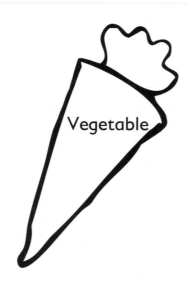

Vegetable

carrot

Weather

2 Look at the words on page 58. Write each word under the correct group name.

Sport

Seaside

Transport

How much did you do?   Activities 1–2

Circle the star to show what you have done.

 Some

 Most

All

More than one

1 When there is more than one of something, we usually add s to the end of the word. Add s to each word. Then write out the word twice.

scooter

balloon

monster

present

2 We usually add es to a word that ends with a hissing or buzzing sound (s, x, sh and ch). Add es to each word. Then write out the word twice.

dress

box

brush

sandwich

watch

3 For words that end in ay, ey or oy, we add s if there is more than one.
Add s to each word.

Parent tip
Call out words and ask your child to write down the plurals. Include some words that end in y.

toy

donkey

4 For words that end in a consonant and the letter y, we change the y to ies if there is more than one. Copy each word twice.

flies

stories

jellies

puppies

cities

families

cherries

fairies

How much did you do?   Activities 1–4

Circle the star to show what you have done.

Some

Most

All

Handwriting practice: 'When I went out for a walk one day'

1 Copy this poem in your neatest handwriting.

When I went out for a walk one day,

My head fell off and rolled away,

And when I saw that it was gone –

I picked it up and put it on.

2 Copy the rest of the poem in your neatest handwriting.

When I went into the street

Someone shouted, 'Look at your feet!'

I looked at them and sadly said,

'I've left them both asleep in bed!'

Anon

Parent tip
Use the progress certificate at the back of this book to make a reward chart for your child.

How much did you do? Activities 1–2

Circle the star to show what you have done.

 Some

 Most

 All

Check your progress

- Shade in the stars on the progress certificate to show how much you did. Shade one star for every ⭐ you circled in this book.
- If you have shaded fewer than 20 stars go back to the pages where you circled Some ☆ or Most ☆ and try those pages again.
- If you have shaded 20 or more stars, well done!

Did you find and colour all 31 monkeys?

(Including this one!)

Collins Easy Learning Handwriting Ages 5–7 bumper book

Progress certificate

name _____

to

date _____

pages 4–5	pages 6–7	pages 8–9	pages 10–11	pages 12–13	pages 14–15	pages 16–17	pages 18–19	pages 20–21	pages 22–23	pages 24–25	pages 26–27	pages 28–29	pages 30–31	pages 32–33
☆1	☆2	☆3	☆4	☆5	☆6	☆7	☆8	☆9	☆10	☆11	☆12	☆13	☆14	☆15
pages 34–35	pages 36–37	pages 38–39	pages 40–41	pages 42–43	pages 44–45	pages 46–47	pages 48–49	pages 50–51	pages 52–53	pages 54–55	pages 56–57	pages 58–59	pages 60–61	pages 62–63
☆16	☆17	☆18	☆19	☆20	☆21	☆22	☆23	☆24	☆25	☆26	☆27	☆28	☆29	☆30